The Kind Servant

A joyful poem about 'Abdu'l-Bahá

Printed by IngramSpark in the United States of America.

ISBN: 978-1-7366095-0-7 (Hardcover)

Book design by Celeste Finn.

First printing, 2021.

Shininglamppress.com

Published in commemoration
of the Centenary
of 'Abdu'l-Bahá's passing.

Who was 'Abdu'l-Bahá?

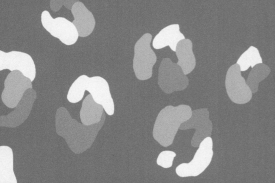

He wore long robes
that flowed in the wind.

He had a fez on His head
and a beard on His chin.

A twinkle in His eye
and brown, sun-kissed skin.

He led the Bahá'í Faith
and called Himself a Servant.
A kind Servant of God,
to whose laws He was observant.

"Be kind to everyone,"
'Abdu'l-Bahá smiled and said.[1]
He was loving and caring
to help happiness spread!

The eldest Son of Baha'u'llah
and generous every day,
He was the Perfect Example
of how to live and pray.

He gave coats to the poor
and made sure they were fed.
He gave what was needed,
like His clothes and His bread!

Early Friday mornings,
a hundred or more
of Akka's poorest humans
would come to His door.

He gave them a pat on the back,
said, "Well done! Well done!"
Then placed a few coins
in the palm of each one.

"Be kind to everyone,"
'Abdu'l-Bahá smiled and said.
He was loving and caring
to help happiness spread!

'Abdu'l-Bahá loved laughter,
praying, and riding His horse.
Also swimming, flowers,
and His cute cat of course![2]

He beamed when children
would run, giggle, and play!
And He loved it when
His grandson Shoghi would pray.

To spread love and joy
at the start of each Feast,
He gave all the children
a yummy, sweet treat.

"Be kind to everyone,"
'Abdu'l-Bahá smiled and said.
He was loving and caring
to help happiness spread!

In God's garden, you're
a strong growing plant.
His prayers are for you!
Here's one you can chant:

O Lord!
Plant this tender seedling
in the garden of Thy manifold
bounties, water it from
the fountains of Thy loving-kindness
and grant that it may grow
into a goodly plant
through the outpourings
of Thy favour and grace.
Thou art the Mighty and the Powerful.[3]

"Be kind to everyone,"
'Abdu'l-Bahá smiled and said.
He was loving and caring
to help happiness spread!

Bibliography

1. Honnold, Annamarie, and 'Abdu'l-Bahá. "Vignettes: from the Life of 'Abdu'l-Bahá." (Oxford: George Ronald, 1997) pg. 39.
2. Rutstein, Nathan. "He Loved and Served: The Story of Curtis Kelsey." (Oxford: George Ronald, 1982).
3. 'Abdu'l-Bahá. "Additional Prayers Revealed by 'Abdu'l-Bahá," Bahá'í Reference Library, Accessed March 12, 2021, http://www.bahai.org/r/653107427.

Photo Source: National Bahá'í Archives, United States

CPSIA information can be obtained
at www.ICGtesting.com
Printed in the USA
BVHW021952250621
610446BV00002B/142